Benjamin Franklin

by Marion Dane Bauer
Illustrated by Anthony Lewis

SCHOLASTIC INC.
New York   Toronto   London   Auckland
Sydney   Mexico City   New Delhi   Hong Kong

ISBN 978-0-545-23256-2

Text copyright © 2010 by Marion Dane Bauer
Illustrations copyright © 2010 by Anthony Lewis

12 11 10 9 8 7 6 5 4 3   11 12 13 14 15 16/0
Printed in the U.S.A.   40
First printing, March 2011

Book design by Jennifer Rinaldi Windau

Benjamin Franklin was born into a large family.
Not even his sixteen brothers and sisters knew
what an amazing man he would be.

Because his father was poor,
Ben had to leave school at age ten.

He had completed only two years of study.

He went to work for his brother as a printer,
but he never stopped learning.

In his spare time, he read and practiced writing.

As a young man, he wrote a popular pamphlet
called *Poor Richard's Almanac*.

The cat in gloves catches no mice.

Fish and visitors stink after three days.

s a
earned.

It was filled with facts and wise sayings like
"An apple a day keeps the doctor away."

North

Sun

West

East

South

12
13
14
15
16
17
18
19
20
21
22
23
24
25
26
27
28

Poor Richard, 1739.
AN
Almanack

Benjamin Franklin loved to perform scientific experiments.

He chased storms on horseback to find out how they moved.

Little was known about electricity in Franklin's time.
No one had even imagined electric lights yet.

But Ben Franklin came up with a daring experiment.

A silk kite flown in a gathering storm could draw electricity from the clouds.

Once he knew for certain that lightning was electricity, he invented lightning rods to keep the bolts from striking buildings.

He even used electricity to ring bells and
to make an artificial spider move!

Benjamin Franklin invented many useful objects like bifocal glasses and the Franklin stove.

He invented swim flippers, too!

He helped set up the first volunteer fire company.

He supported a free school for poor children
and the first lending library.

And while he did all these things, he worked long and hard to help the United States of America become an independent nation.

The Signing of the Declaration of Independence, 1776

The Constitutional Convention, 1787

This country has many founding fathers.
Benjamin Franklin was one of the
most amazing.

He spent his entire life learning and discovering
and making a better world.